The Little Book of Small World Play

A world in your hand!

Written by
Sharon Ward
Edited by Sally Featherstone
Illustrations by Kerry Ingham

LITTLE BOOKS WITH **BIG** IDEAS

This edition published 2013 by Featherstone, an imprint of Bloomsbury Publishing Plc
Published 2005 by A&C Black, an imprint of Bloomsbury Publishing Plc
50 Bedford Square, London WC1B 3DP
www.bloomsbury.com

ISBN 978-1-4729-0350-1

Text © Sharon Ward, 2005
Illustrations © Kerry Ingham, 2005
Series Editor, Sally Featherstone

A CIP record for this publication is available from the British Library.

Printed and bound in India by Replika Press Pvt. Ltd.

This book is produced using paper that is made from wood grown in
managed, sustainable forests. It is natural, renewable and recyclable.

The logging and manufacturing processes conform to the environmental
regulations of the country of origin.

10 9 8 7 6 5 4 3 2 1

**To see our full range of titles
visit www.bloomsbury.com**

Contents

Introduction

This book is one of the titles in a series of Little Books, which explore aspects of practice within the Early Years Foundation Stage in England. The books are also suitable for practitioners working with the early years curriculum in Wales, Northern Ireland and Scotland, and in any early years setting catering for young children.

Across the series you will find titles appropriate to each aspect of the curriculum for children from two to five years, giving practitioners a wealth of ideas for engaging activities, interesting resources and stimulating environments to enrich their work across the Early Years Curriculum. Outdoor play should be a daily activity, and free access to an outdoor area is an ideal we should all work towards.

Each title also has information linking the activity pages to the statutory Early Years curriculum for England. This title has been updated to include the revised Early Learning Goals published by the Department for Education in March 2012. The full set of 19 goals is included in the introduction to each book, and the activity pages will refer you to the relevant statements to which each activity contributes.

For the purposes of observation and assessment of the children's work in each activity, we recommend that practitioners should use each of the 'revised statements' as a whole, resisting any impulse to separate the elements of each one into short phrases.

The key goals for this title are highlighted in blue, although other goals may be included on some pages.

PRIME AREAS

Communication and language

1 Listening and attention: children listen attentively in a range of situations. They listen to stories, accurately anticipating key events and respond to what they hear with relevant comments, questions or actions. They give their attention to what others say and respond appropriately, while engaged in another activity.

2 Understanding: children follow instructions involving several ideas or actions. They answer 'how' and 'why' questions about their experiences and in response to stories or events.

3 Speaking: children express themselves effectively, showing awareness of listeners' needs. They use past, present and future forms accurately when talking about events that have happened or are to happen in the future. They develop their own narratives and explanations by connecting ideas or events.

Physical development

1 Moving and handling: children show good control and co-ordination in large and small movements. They move confidently in a range of ways, safely negotiating space. They handle equipment and tools effectively, including pencils for writing.

2 **Health and self-care:** children know the importance for good health of physical exercise, and a healthy diet, and talk about ways to keep healthy and safe. They manage their own basic hygiene and personal needs successfully, including dressing and going to the toilet independently.

Personal, social and emotional development

1 **Self-confidence and self-awareness:** children are confident to try new activities, and say why they like some activities more than others. They are confident to speak in a familiar group, will talk about their ideas, and will choose the resources they need for their chosen activities. They say when they do or don't need help.

2 **Managing feelings and behaviour:** children talk about how they and others show feelings, talk about their own and others' behaviour, and its consequences, and know that some behaviour is unacceptable. They work as part of a group or class, and understand and follow the rules. They adjust their behaviour to different situations, and take changes of routine in their stride.

3 **Making relationships:** children play co-operatively, taking turns with others. They take account of one another's ideas about how to organise their activity. They show sensitivity to others' needs and feelings, and form positive relationships with adults and other children.

SPECIFIC AREAS

Literacy

1 **Reading:** children read and understand simple sentences. They use phonic knowledge to decode regular words and read them aloud accurately. They also read some common irregular words. They demonstrate understanding when talking with others about what they have read.

2 **Writing:** children use their phonic knowledge to write words in ways which match their spoken sounds. They also write some irregular common words. They write simple sentences which can be read by themselves and others. Some words are spelt correctly and others are phonetically plausible.

Mathematics

1 **Numbers:** children count reliably with numbers from 1 to 20, place them in order and say which number is one more or one less than a given number. Using quantities and objects, they add and subtract two single-digit numbers and count on or back to find the answer. They solve problems, including doubling, halving and sharing.

2 **Shape, space and measures:** children use everyday language to talk about size, weight, capacity, position, distance, time and money to compare quantities and objects and to solve problems. They recognise, create and describe patterns. They explore characteristics of everyday objects and shapes and use mathematical language to describe them.

Understanding the world

(1) People and communities: children talk about past and present events in their own lives and in the lives of family members. They know that other children don't always enjoy the same things, and are sensitive to this. They know about similarities and differences between themselves and others, and among families, communities and traditions.

(2) The world: children know about similarities and differences in relation to places, objects, materials and living things. They talk about the features of their own immediate environment and how environments might vary from one another. They make observations of animals and plants and explain why some things occur, and talk about changes.

(3) Technology: children recognise that a range of technology is used in places such as homes and schools. They select and use technology for particular purposes.

Expressive arts and design

(1) Exploring and using media and materials: children sing songs, make music and dance, and experiment with ways of changing them. They safely use and explore a variety of materials, tools and techniques, experimenting with colour, design, texture, form and function.

(2) Being imaginative: children use what they have learnt about media and materials in original ways, thinking about uses and purposes. They represent their own ideas, thoughts and feelings through design and technology, art, music, dance, role-play and stories.

Major contribution of the activities to Early Learning Goals

PRIME

Communication and Language

Physical Development (1)

Personal, social and emotional development (1) (3)

SPECIFIC

Mathematics (2)

Understanding of the World (1) (2)

Expressive arts and design 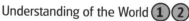 (1) (2)

Introduction

Well-planned play

Small world play activities provide opportunities for learning both indoors and outdoors. Play activities help children to learn with both enjoyment and challenge. Through play activities, such as small world play activities, children can:

▶ explore, develop and represent learning experiences that help them make sense of the world;

▶ practise and build up ideas, concepts and skills;

▶ be alone, be alongside others or co-operate as they talk or rehearse their feelings;

▶ take risks and make mistakes;

▶ think creatively and imaginatively;

▶ communicate with others as they investigate or solve problems;

▶ express fears or relive anxious experiences in controlled and safe situations. (Taken from 'Curriculum Guidance for the Foundation Stage', DFES, 2000)

All the activities in this book can be adapted to suit your setting and the topics you are covering. Collecting your own resources for the activities and exploring them with your children will give as much pleasure as using them in adult-directed activities.

Addressing the principles of the Early Years Foundation Stage Curriculum through small world play activities

Effective education requires both a relevant curriculum and practitioners who understand and are able to implement curriculum requirements. Small world play can be topic-based or can be used as an exploration activity. The activities promote social interaction and there are many cross-curricular links within one activity.

Effective education requires practitioners who understand that children develop rapidly during the Early Years – physically, intellectually, emotionally and socially. Small world activities can support and extend children's knowledge and skills, and small world play aids the development of fine motor control. Children are also learning and exploring in a non-threatening way alongside their peers.

Parents and practitioners should work together. Parents can help with donating resources. Share the small world by setting up one of the activities during an open day or parents' evening.

No child should be excluded or disadvantaged. Small world activities can be accessed by every child in your setting and
can help to raise awareness of different cultures and religions.

To be effective, an Early Years curriculum should be carefully structured. Children can use the small world activities as a starting point to develop their own ideas. Children will gain different skills and knowledge from the small world activities depending on their ability. Children can access the small world at their own level. Planned small world activities provide opportunities for teaching and learning inside the classroom and in your outdoor area.

Early Years experience should build on what the children already know and can do. Small world play activities naturally extend and build on children's early knowledge.

Practitioners should ensure that all children feel included, secure and valued. Small world play activities are aimed at all children in your setting, allowing all individuals to feel included. Children should feel confident to make suggestions for developments to the small worlds.

There should be opportunities for children to engage in activities planned by adults and also those that they plan or initiate themselves. Through a small world activity, children are given time to explore and initiate their own ideas, using the structure of the activity as a starting point for learning.

Practitioners must be able to observe and respond appropriately to children. An adult can work alongside children to model, respond to, and extend ideas with the children through the small world play activity. Observation of such play enables practitioners to recognise learning and plan for the next steps.

Well-planned, purposeful activity and appropriate intervention by practitioners will engage children in the learning process. The ideas in this book are well planned, linked to the Early Learning Goals, and aim to engage children and their imaginations.

For children to have rich and stimulating experiences, the learning environment should be well planned and well organised. The small world play activities in this book provide a structure for teaching in which children are able to explore, experiment, plan and make decisions. Through these activities, they will learn, develop, make good progress and gain confidence.

Above all, effective learning and development for young children requires high-quality care and education by practitioners. Small world play activities provide high-quality learning opportunities for all children in a variety of Early Years settings.

Dinosaur World

Focus: Step back in time and enjoy the experience of a different world.

What you need:

> I will need

- a selection of small plastic dinosaurs
- a large plastic tray, for example, a builder's tray or the lid to a sandpit/water tray
- plastic plants, for example fish tank greenery or model railway trees
- a selection of small stones
- four or five pints (2 litres) of lime jelly (depending on the size of the tray).

Contribution to Early Learning Goals for the EYFS

PRIME

Communication and Language ① ③

Physical Development ①

PSED ① ③

SPECIFIC

Mathematics ②

Understanding the world ① ②

Expressive arts and design ① ②

What to do:

Preparation

▶ Let the children help you to make the lime jelly in a bucket or big bowl the day before you want to set up the small world. Explain to them what you are going to do and keep them well away from the hot water.

▶ Empty the set jelly into the middle of the large tray.

▶ Arrange the stones and plants around the outside of the tray.

▶ Add the dinosaurs to the tray and you are ready for play.

Independent exploration

▶ Introduce and talk about the small world during group time and encourage the children to explore it independently.

EXPLAIN THAT THE JELLY IS NOT FOR EATING, AS THERE MAY BE GERMS IN IT FROM CHILDREN'S HANDS!

Ideas for adult-initiated activities:

▶ Look at pictures and books about dinosaurs and try to identify the names of the plastic ones.

▶ Talk about how to make jelly and other materials that can be changed. For example, making water into ice or melting chocolate.

▶ Describe the sounds that are made when the dinosaurs travel through the jelly.

▶ Count the dinosaurs, sort them into groups or use them to explore number bonds and simple addition and subtraction problems. For example, 'if there are two dinosaurs playing and another one comes to join them, how many dinosaurs will we have altogether?'

▶ Use positional language to describe where the dinosaurs are, for example, 'the green one is behind the red one'.

Key words

dinosaur	fly	runny	vegetation
names	meat eater	lumpy	rocks
prehistoric	plant eater	set	swamp
extinct	fierce	melt	smooth
spikes	scared	investigate	squelch

Troll Forest

Focus: Enter the crazy world of trolls and make your mark!

What you need:

- a selection of different sized troll dolls (try charity shops or car boot sales!)
- brightly coloured/multi-coloured material/fabric/card
- a selection of different types of sticky notes, including speech bubble ones
- coloured pencils, construction materials/junk modelling
- clipboards.

Contribution to Early Learning Goals for the EYFS

PRIME

Communication and Language ① ③

Physical Development ①

PSED ① ③

SPECIFIC

Mathematics ②

Understanding the world ① ②

Expressive arts and design ① ②

What to do:

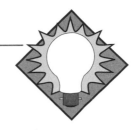

Preparation

▶ Cover a table top with the fabric/card.

▶ Lay the trolls out on the table.

▶ Put the sticky notes, pencils, clipboards and pencils close by.

Independent exploration

▶ Remember how important it is to start with exploration and free play with new materials. Introduce the troll world and give the children plenty of uninterrupted time to play with the trolls and make their own stories and environments.

Ideas for adult-initiated activities:

▶ Make up some stories with the children by choosing a troll and introducing your character to the children. Don't be embarrassed to talk in a 'character' voice – the children will love it!

▶ Sort the trolls according to colour/size/dress etc.

▶ Use speech bubble sticky notes to create a story using the trolls as characters. These could be scribed by an adult or written independently by the children.

▶ Use construction materials/junk modelling to add houses to the troll world. Make name labels and numbers on the houses using small sticky notes.

▶ Record all the colours you can see in the troll land using coloured pencils and a clipboard. Name all the colours.

▶ Talk about primary colours and how to mix secondary colours. Use paints to have a go.

▶ Use this idea to make environments and stories for 'My Little Pony' characters, 'Bob the Builder' or 'Superhero' miniatures.

Key words			
colour words	small	once upon a time	next
primary colours	medium	one day	after
secondary colours	house	happened	beginning
rainbow	house names	happily ever after	end
multi-coloured	troll names	good character	exciting
big	number names	bad character	oh

Reptile World

Focus: Explore this sandy world and learn about reptiles.

What you need:

I will need

- ▶ a selection of plastic lizards, frogs, snakes etc.
- ▶ silver sand
- ▶ a builder's tray or large plastic lid
- ▶ a small pot of water
- ▶ plastic vegetation.

Contribution to Early Learning Goals for the EYFS

PRIME

Communication and Language ① ③

Physical Development ①

PSED ① ③

SPECIFIC

Mathematics ②

Understanding the world ① ②

Expressive arts and design ① ②

What to do:

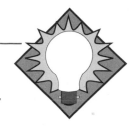

Preparation

▶ Put a thick layer of sand in the tray (enough to make mounds, caves, tunnels etc.)

▶ Add the reptile figures.

▶ Put the plastic vegetation somewhere near.

▶ Add a small pot or saucer of water for the reptiles to drink from.

Independent exploration

▶ Introduce the activity and talk about it with the children. Allow time for independent exploration. This stage needs plenty of time.

Ideas for adult-initiated activities:

▶ Play alongside the children, talking about what the reptiles are, where they live, and what they eat and do.

▶ Look closely at the different reptiles, their colours, patterns, shapes and sizes. Sort them into reptiles that live in different places – hot and dry, wet and boggy, and under water.

▶ Take a trip to your book corner, school library or public library for books, posters and other information to help you to identify different reptiles, their names, habitats and needs.

▶ Use Google to find hundreds of reptile pictures.

▶ Talk about the texture of the sand and compare it with other textures.

▶ Talk with the children about reptile diets and life cycles.

▶ Compare the reptile world with our own environment; talk about similarities and differences.

▶ Use an atlas to locate hot and cold countries, or an animal atlas to locate where different reptiles live.

▶ Find out about British reptiles, such as frogs, toads, snakes and lizards.

Key words			
reptile names	rough	lizard	sun
desert	vegetation	egg	heat
hot	frog	tadpole	
dry	toad	water	
sand	snake	land	

If You Go Down to the Woods

Focus: ... you're sure of a big surprise!

What you need:

I will need

- ▶ a selection of woodland finger puppets or small toys, such as bears, rabbits, badgers, squirrels, deer, foxes etc.
- ▶ a builder's tray or another large tray
- ▶ paper or fabric with leaves printed on
- ▶ a doll's tea set and small size plastic food (try a 'bargain' or doll's house shop)
- ▶ a tape recorder/CD player
- ▶ song tapes/CDs and blank tapes
- ▶ a selection of musical instruments or familiar objects that can be used as sound makers (for example, bubble wrap, combs etc.).

Contribution to Early Learning Goals for the EYFS

PRIME

Communication and Language ① ③

Physical Development ①

PSED ① ③

SPECIFIC

Mathematics ②

Understanding the world ① ②

Expressive arts and design ① ②

What to do:

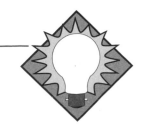

Preparation

▶ Lay the paper or fabric inside the builder's tray.

▶ Add the puppets/toys.

▶ Arrange the tea set and play food in the tray.

▶ Set up the tape recorder/CD player and musical instruments next to the small world.

▶ Children could make some tiny food with baked and painted clay or dough.

Independent exploration

▶ Introduce and talk about the small world during group time and encourage the children to explore it independently. Let them explore the woodland tea party first, adding new items they have made or found, and getting to know the different animals.

▶ When they have had time to explore the setting, add some musical opportunities – appropriate songs such as 'The Teddy Bears' Picnic', or some simple instruments and sound makers to add to their play. Sit with the children and follow their lead.

Ideas for adult-initiated activities:

▶ Read 'The Happy Hedgehog Band' (Martin Waddell, Candlewick Press). Talk about the band in the wood and replay the story with puppets or other figures (they don't need to all be hedgehogs) or just with musical accompaniment.

▶ Sing along to a variety of themed songs, for example, 'If you go down to the woods today...' and 'Teddy bear, teddy bear.'

▶ Encourage the children to make their own songs about the animals using the instruments.

▶ Record the children singing and making music onto blank tapes to listen to later.

Key words

animal names	loud	rattle	sound
names of the instruments	quiet	start	noise
	shake	stop	beat
	bang	play	story
	tap	record	

Our Class

Focus: **A small world full of familiar faces.**

What you need:

- ▶ a digital camera
- ▶ a laminator
- ▶ small wooden construction bricks (3–4cm/2" cubes)
- ▶ large sheets of paper, felt pens, scissors, fabric scraps and card
- ▶ small construction boxes e.g. food boxes
- ▶ wax crayons.

Contribution to Early Learning Goals for the EYFS

PRIME

Communication and Language ① ③

Physical Development ①

PSED ① ③

SPECIFIC

Mathematics ②

Understanding the world ① ②

Expressive arts and design ① ②

What to do:

Preparation

▶ Take individual photos of each child in the class; you can either just do the faces, or the whole body (this is more fun for the children!). Include yourself and other familiar adults if possible.

▶ Print the photos small size. 8–10cm tall is a good size.

▶ Laminate them if possible. This will make them last longer and stand up better. If you haven't got access to a laminator, use clear sticky plastic. Children can then cut their figures out to use for play.

▶ Help the children to stick the cut-out photos on small construction bricks so they can stand up.

▶ Lay out large sheets of paper and put the construction materials, pens etc. where the children can get them.

Independent exploration

▶ Talk with the children about making an environment for their figures – they may choose to make a classroom, a playground, a house – follow their lead.

▶ Talk about the construction materials and how the children can make them into houses, furniture, toys etc.

▶ Help them if they need it. You could also work alongside them, making your own objects and talking about what you are doing.

▶ Use crayons or felt pens to draw features on the big sheets of paper – carpets for indoors, paths and grass for a park, sand, rocks and pools for a seaside visit.

Ideas for adult-initiated activities:

▶ Use the photo figures to explore personal and social situations such as friendship problems, feelings of isolation, sharing, bullying, telling a teacher if someone hurts you and not fighting back etc.

▶ Children will love using the figures to retell things that have happened to them at home and in your setting.

Key words

sharing	sad	right	together
friends	upset	wrong	funny
alone	angry	problem	laugh
lonely	hurt	difficult	work
happy	confused	talk	

Under the Sea

Focus: Step back in time and enjoy the experience of a different world.

What you need:

- a builder's tray or equivalent (an empty aquarium is ideal for this!)
- mermaid dolls, or other appropriate dolls, such as divers or swimmers
- blue and green shredded paper, tissue, cellophane and foil
- coloured sequins and ribbons
- small shells, aquarium rocks, plastic fish etc.
- a CD player and sea music (try a wave music CD).

Contribution to Early Learning Goals for the EYFS

PRIME

Communication and Language ① ③
Physical Development ①
PSED ① ③

SPECIFIC

Mathematics ②
Understanding the world ① ②
Expressive arts and design ① ②

What to do:

Preparation

▶ Shred the paper in a shredder or with scissors, or let the children shred strips themselves (much more fun).

▶ Fill up the tray or aquarium with the shreddings for water.

▶ Sprinkle in some sequins.

▶ Add the dolls and shells.

▶ Set up the CD player next to the small world and offer some CDs for the children to accompany their play.

Independent exploration

▶ Talk about the water world with the children, and discuss the different stories and scenes they could invent.

▶ Give plenty of time for independent play before introducing directed activities.

▶ Invite the children to bring other small items from home to share in the play.

Ideas for adult-initiated activities:

▶ Ask the children to close their eyes while you listen to some calm sea music, then talk about the pictures they see in their heads.

▶ Sing songs about the sea and the seaside, read stories about the sea ('Lucy and Tom', 'Sally and the Limpet', 'Miffy, Master Salt the sailor's son', 'Rainbow Fish' etc.).

▶ Think of words to describe the sea on a summer day, or on a stormy winter day.

▶ Tell an underwater adventure story and act it out.

▶ Make sea pictures using the colours from the small world.

▶ Use white crayon or a candle to make wax-resistant pictures. Draw the picture, then paint over with very thin blue paint to see the picture emerge like magic.

Key words

mermaid	waves	shimmer	scales
sea	ripple	swim	
calm	tide	dive	
blue	rough	float	
green	stormy	tail	

Down on the Farm

Focus: Enjoy exploring this busy small world.

What you need:

▶ a builder's tray or equivalent shallow container

▶ farmyard animal figures: sheep, cows, ducks, chickens, horses, pigs etc.

▶ small people, farmer, farmer's wife, shepherd, tractor driver, children etc.

▶ greengrocer's grass (ask your local greengrocer or put 'display grass' in Google to find addresses)

▶ blue plastic or an unbreakable mirror for a pond, plastic trees, greenery (plastic fish tank plants are ideal) and recycled materials for construction.

Contribution to Early Learning Goals for the EYFS

PRIME

Communication and Language ① ③

Physical Development ①

PSED ① ③

SPECIFIC

Mathematics ②

Understanding the world ① ②

Expressive arts and design ① ②

22

What to do:

Preparation
▶ Lay the greengrocer's grass in the bottom of the tray.
▶ Gather all the other resources in a box next to the tray.
▶ Involve the children in setting up the small world, making the farmhouse, fences, hen house etc., from boxes and other recycled materials.
▶ Arrange the plants and trees around the tray.
▶ Put the animals and people into their part of the small world.

Independent exploration
▶ You could start this small world focus with a country or farming story such as 'Spot at the Farm', 'Sheep in a Jeep', 'Fix it Duck', 'Farmer Duck', 'Duck in a Truck', 'Pig in the Pond' etc.
▶ Give the children plenty of time to explore the small world and use their imagination to make up or retell stories using the people, vehicles and animals.

Ideas for adult-initiated activities:
▶ Sing 'Old Macdonald Had a Farm', using the animal figures as prompts.
▶ Make some field with bricks or fences and sort the animals. Ask older children addition and subtraction problems using the animals. For example, 'If we have five sheep and one got lost, how many sheep would we have left?'
▶ Use the figures to develop positional language, for example, 'Put the hen house next to the pond' and 'Put the pig behind the tree'.
▶ Discuss the food we get from farms, how and where it grows, and how it gets to the shops.
▶ Match the animals to their babies, the food they eat and where they live.
▶ Make a list of all the jobs the farmer might have to do in a day.
▶ Discuss how the seasons might affect the farm and how it looks at different times of the year.

Key words

animal names	grass	number names	tractor
spring	trees	behind	plough
summer	fields	in front	food
autumn	fence	gate	
winter	house	barn	

Pigs in Mud

Focus: Wallow around in this small world.

What you need:

- ▶ a builder's tray or another large shallow tray
- ▶ compost (a growbag is a cheap way to get compost, but avoid ones with a high proportion of peat)
- ▶ plastic pig figures
- ▶ access to water.

Contribution to Early Learning Goals for the EYFS

PRIME

Communication and Language ① ③

Physical Development ①

PSED ① ③

SPECIFIC

Mathematics ②

Understanding the world ① ②

Expressive arts and design ① ②

What to do:

Preparation

▶ Ask the children to help you to fill the tray with compost.

▶ Arrange the pigs inside the tray.

▶ Add some water for immediate messy play or have a small container of water nearby to allow children to experiment.

▶ Read a suitable story, such as 'The Pig in the Pond' or 'Mrs Wishy Washy'.

Independent exploration

▶ Let the children explore the play situation. It will be messy, even before they add the water, so you could do this outside.

▶ Join the children as they play, watch and listen, but don't be tempted to interrupt their flow with your ideas.

▶ Play alongside if this seems appropriate, but **never** imply that you don't like messy play by your actions, expressions or words.

Ideas for adult-initiated activities:

▶ Think of words to describe the sound, smell and texture of the mud.

▶ Talk about how materials and substances change when you add water. Try mixing other things such as paint, cornflour, coffee and sugar, and discuss where the materials go when/if they disappear. Use words like 'dissolve', 'disappear', 'mixture'.

Ask the children whether the mixture can be separated out again – can you get the sugar back? – How would you do it. Leave some of the mixtures in a warm place and watch what happens as the water evaporates. You could leave the pig mud outside overnight and see what happens.

▶ Talk about animals and their young. Practise using the right names and putting pictures or animals in families.

▶ Make more 'wet worlds' for model ducks, geese and pond creatures.

Key words			
wet	thick	lumpy	pig/piglet
water	oozy	dirty	sheep/lamb
dry	squelch	dissolve	cow/calf
mud	squirch	disappear	duck/duckling
runny	smooth	mixture	

On the Moon

Focus: Use simple imaginative materials for an 'out of the world' experience.

What you need:

I will need

▶ a builder's tray or equivalent shallow tray

▶ slime or cornflour (try colouring this with blue or green food colouring)

▶ small vehicles, small people figures (preferably spacemen!) and alien figures

▶ books and pictures about space

▶ telescopes and rockets (made from cardboard tubes)

▶ clipboards and pencils.

Contribution to Early Learning Goals for the EYFS

PRIME

Communication and Language ①③

Physical Development ①

PSED ①③

SPECIFIC

Mathematics ②

Understanding the world ①②

Expressive arts and design ①②

What to do:

Preparation

▶ Have a session making rockets, spacecraft and telescopes with the children using boxes and cardboard tubes.

▶ Cover the base of the tray with a small layer of cornflour or slime.

▶ Help the children to arrange the people, aliens, rockets and moon buggies inside the tray.

▶ Put the books, pictures and telescopes near the tray for reference.

Independent exploration

▶ Introduce the activity through relevant stories, songs and poems. Look for some simple fact books about night, space exploration and astronauts.

▶ Let the children have plenty of free exploration time before embarking on using the small world as a teaching tool.

Ideas for adult-initiated activities:

▶ Use pictures and books to talk about space exploration and going to the Moon.

▶ Have a conversation about aliens! Explore the concepts of real, pretend, imagined, and of real life and stories. Remember that young children have a real problem with this and may not be able to accept that some things they see (especially on TV) are not real. Dressing up, making masks and small worlds are good ways to explore these concepts, but don't expect immediate acceptance and understanding.

▶ Talk about near and far away, how long it takes to get to the Moon, or the stars. Use the Internet to download pictures from space.

▶ Watch a short film clip of moon landings or space exploration and do some role play as astronauts. Use Google or the NASA website to find space photos.

Key words

space	sun	rocket	gravity
moon	stars	space shuttle	telescope
names of the planets	universe	zoom	
	galaxy	alien	
astronaut	buggy	atmosphere	

Arctic Adventure

Focus: Put on your gloves and explore this small world.

What you need:

▶ a builder's tray or another large shallow tray

▶ ice cube trays, pudding basins, plastic pots, cups and tubs

▶ plastic arctic and sea creatures – whales, dolphins, seals, sea lions, penguins and polar bears; small world people and sledges (or materials to make them)

▶ cornflour, sequins, small beads, seeds etc.

Contribution to Early Learning Goals for the EYFS

PRIME

Communication and Language ① ③

Physical Development ①

PSED ① ③

SPECIFIC

Mathematics ②

Understanding the world ① ②

Expressive arts and design ① ②

What to do:

Preparation

▶ Let the children help you to fill the containers and ice cube trays with water, and put them in the freezer overnight.

▶ Empty the ice into the tray and scatter cornflour over the top.

▶ Add some sequins, beads or seeds to the tray and put the creatures and other figures nearby. Don't be tempted to set the scene up for the children!

Independent exploration

▶ Children may need gloves for this small world, especially in winter or out of doors. Check frequently to make sure they are warm enough, but otherwise, just let them experience the materials and figures, watching as the ice melts.

Ideas for adult-initiated activities:

▶ Read some stories about snowy, icy places – 'Pingu', 'Tacky the Penguin', 'The Little Polar Bear', 'Boy and a Bear', 'The Last Polar Bears', 'The Storm Seal' and 'Sammythe Seal'.

▶ Talk about freezing and melting and the processes involved.

▶ Name the creatures and think about what they eat. Look for cold countries on a map or globe. Remember that polar bears come from the North Pole and penguins from the South Pole.

▶ Make ice cubes with the children to be used the next day. Ask the children to find small objects around the classroom to freeze inside the ice cubes or sprinkle sequins into the ice cube trays.

▶ Compare the small world with the children's own environment. Talk to the children about what they like or dislike about the two different environments.

▶ When you have finished with the small world, put any remaining lumps of ice on the plant pots in your setting to water the plants.

Key words			
freeze	melt	animal names	float
freezing	solid	sparkle	sink
ice	liquid	glitter	
iceberg	shape	North Pole	
water	hard/soft	South Pole	

Our Town

Focus: Create your own town, village or setting in this small world development.

What you need:

I will need

▶ a road map made of plastic or a big piece of carpet

▶ small world people and small vehicles

▶ road signs (make some with the children) with lolly sticks, playdough, paper circles and triangles and pictures of road signs (enter 'road signs' into Google Images for free road sign pictures to print and use.)

▶ construction kits such as Lego, or big wooden bricks

▶ sticky notes and pencils.

Contribution to Early Learning Goals for the EYFS

PRIME

Communication and Language ① ③

Physical Development ①

PSED ① ③

SPECIFIC

Mathematics ②

Understanding the world ① ②

Expressive arts and design ① ②

What to do:

Preparation

▶ The road mats available to buy are often disappointing for children because they are small and difficult to use for a realistic road map. If you want a bigger one, make your own. Buy a remnant of carpet and paint roads and footpaths on it with emulsion paint. Then it will fit the buildings and cars you have or the ones the children make.

▶ You could take the children on a local walk and make a realistic layout with parks, shops etc. and even the streets where the children live.

▶ Or, you could use playground chalk to make a road or town map outside on a path or patio.

▶ Let the children help with making road signs, buildings, car parks and bus stops from recycled materials. (Use free symbols from the Internet or copy some from a Highway Code.)

Independent exploration

▶ Play alongside the children as they construct the layout, making buildings and designing other parts of the scene. Use photos of local places to help them with their construction. Don't try to make the model realistic in scale, it will frustrate you and the children won't worry about inconsistencies.

Ideas for adult-initiated activities:

▶ Look at photos of streets, parks, buildings and shops and – talk about the ones they know.

▶ Download an aerial photo of your local area from Google Earth and look at your place from the air.

▶ Encourage the children to describe journeys using the small world people and roads.

▶ Make labels and signs for the buildings.

▶ Develop this small world further by removing the map and challenging the children to make a new place with roads, parks, houses and shops.

Key words			
road	cinema	station	in between
street	bank	left/right	past
pavement	garage	forwards	traffic lights
path	petrol	turn	stop/wait
house	car/bus	roundabout	go
shop	train	next to	crossing

Pet Place

Focus: Looking after pets helps children to understand how to look after others.

What you need:

I will need

▶ a pet carrying box or large tray or a small cat/dog basket

▶ sawdust

▶ a variety of soft pet toys, rabbits, gerbils, mice and hamsters

▶ bowls, a packet of pet food, charts and posters (try www.rspca.org.uk for inexpensive and free stuff)

▶ clipboards, paper and pencils.

Contribution to Early Learning Goals for the EYFS

PRIME

Communication and Language ① ③

Physical Development ①

PSED ① ③

SPECIFIC

Mathematics ②

Understanding the world ① ②

Expressive arts and design ① ②

What to do:

Preparation

▶ Talk with the children about pets and their needs. The children may be able to bring photos of their pets or their own soft animals to add to this activity.

▶ You could put this activity on the floor in a corner so you can display information and books about pets nearby.

▶ Empty the sawdust into the cage or tray, or put a blanket in the basket.

▶ Leave the animals in a basket or box so the children can choose which to care for. Put the food where the children can use it.

▶ Have the clipboards and pencils nearby so the children can record their notes etc.

Independent exploration

▶ Leave the situation for free play, joining the children sometimes to listen to what they know or to model the activity by playing alongside them.

Ideas for adult initiated activities:

▶ When the children have had time to explore the activity, talk about what they know about looking after pets. Encourage the children to talk about their own pets.

▶ Use the clipboards to write labels and instructions for looking after the pets.

▶ Ask the children to choose names for the pets and write name labels for the cages or baskets.

▶ Visit a vet, animal sanctuary, city farm or other place where animals are cared for.

▶ Download some information and activities from RSPCA, PDSA, CDL (dogs), Animal Rescuers (horses and donkeys) and Pet Rescue websites.

Key words

water	rabbit	cat/dog	medicine
food	hamster	pet	injection
care	rat	care	bandage
sawdust	mouse	sick	
gerbil	cage	vet	

Fairy Kingdom

Focus: Create your own fantasy stories in this sparkly world.

What you need:

▶ glitter playdough (see page 63)
▶ small fairy figures (Christmas decorations are great for this)
▶ coloured net material
▶ sequins and sequin waste material
▶ a builder's tray or large plastic tray
▶ different coloured sticky notes, paper and
   pens, a tape recorder and tape.

Contribution to Early Learning Goals for the EYFS

PRIME

Communication and Language ①③
Physical Development ①
PSED ①③

SPECIFIC

Mathematics ②
Understanding the world ①②
Expressive arts and design ①②

What to do:

Preparation
▶ A small group of children can make the dough for this activity.
▶ Place the dough in the tray and put the other materials in baskets beside the tray.

Independent exploration
▶ Introduce the activity to the children. Explain that they can make their fairy land any way they like. Encourage them to add other materials and objects as they play – some may want to add leaves and twigs, feathers and stones. Others may want to use junk materials to make homes and other places for the fairies to live.
▶ Play alongside if the children need some support, but make sure you let them lead the play. Try starting off a story and leaving the children to complete it.

Ideas for adult-initiated activities:
▶ Suggest that the fairy land needs labels and signs. Children could use the sticky notes for these, or make their own with card and small sticks.
▶ You could go on a walk in the park or country and collect natural materials to add to the fairy kingdom. Encourage and support the children to write a story, which describes a day in the life of one of the fairies.
▶ Encourage the children to make up stories about the fairies and the fairies' friends. Record some of these in photo sequences, on tape or video, encouraging the children to operate cameras and tape machines independently.
▶ Play the recorded stories for the children to act out using the fairy figures. Make story books from digital photos taken as the children play their stories.

Key words

fairy	glitter	middle/end	pause
magic	colour words	play/stop	photos
magical	once upon a time	record	
fantasy	happily ever after	fast forward	
story	beginning	rewind	

Russian Dolls

Focus: Explore a set of nesting dolls and learn about size, shape, pattern and position.

What you need:

I will need

- ▶ a selection of the nesting Russian dolls called Matryoshka dolls (look for these in charity shops or on the Internet)
- ▶ a small doll's house
- ▶ fake 'grocers grass' (try www.interiorlandscaping.co.uk for artificial grass)
- ▶ 'The Littlest Matryoshka' story by Corrine Demas (Hyperion Books)
- ▶ pencils and strips of small card.

Contribution to Early Learning Goals for the EYFS

PRIME

Communication and Language ① ③

Physical Development ①

PSED ① ③

SPECIFIC

Mathematics ②

Understanding the world ① ②

Expressive arts and design ① ②

What to do:

Preparation

▶ Read the story together, or make one up, using the set of dolls. 'The Littlest Matryoshka' is about the tiniest doll in a doll set who gets lost – an easy story to replicate, with or without a doll's house.

▶ Make a house from a cardboard box if you haven't got a doll's house. Add furniture or bricks and boxes for chairs and beds.

▶ Lay the grass on a table or the floor and set up the house.

▶ Add the Russian dolls to the world, opening some up.

Independent exploration

▶ Leave the children to explore the dolls and the house. They may retell the story or make up their own. They may also want to add other small world characters and objects to the scene and their stories.

▶ Just having you with them may help them to think and talk about the stories they are making. Try not to influence – ask open questions and make suggestions, but try to listen more than you talk!

Ideas for adult-initiated activities:

▶ Count and order the dolls.

▶ Estimate how many dolls fit into one of the big dolls.

▶ Explore positional language as you describe the positions of dolls.

▶ Make name labels for each of the dolls (you could try using the same initial letter for each doll, changing the letter each day as you write new names).

▶ Find Russia on a globe or map of the world.

▶ Read 'The Littlest Matryoshka' story while the children respond using the dolls. Talk about sisters and being lost in response to the story.

▶ Add Fimbles toys to the small world and read 'Fimbles: Russian Doll' (BBC, Penguin Books).

Key words			
big	small	out	more
bigger	smallest	next to	less
large	empty/full	behind	wood
largest	hollow	in front	pattern
medium	inside	estimate	same
middle	in	guess	different

At the Building Site

Focus: Can you fix this small world?

What you need:

- a builder's tray or equivalent shallow tray
- small stones, gravel and sand
- large polished stones
- small trucks and diggers – Bob the Builder, Playmobil and Lego toys are ideal
- small world people, or Bob the Builder/Lego/Playmobil figures
- construction bricks.

Contribution to Early Learning Goals for the EYFS

PRIME

Communication and Language ① ③

Physical Development ①

PSED ① ③

SPECIFIC

Mathematics ②

Understanding the world ① ②

Expressive arts and design ① ②

What to do:

Preparation

▶ Try to find a building site or road works to visit. Take some photos of the vehicles and workmen for your small world area.

▶ Place the small and large stones into the tray.

▶ Put the vehicles and people in a basket or box by the tray.

▶ Add the construction materials.

▶ Put some books about construction near the play area.

▶ You could supply some child-sized hard hats for wearing during play.

Independent exploration

▶ This play will need no encouragement! Let the children loose and they will have endless fun digging and scooping the materials into lorries, making heaps and holes, burying and uncovering.

Ideas for adult-initiated activities:

▶ Read some 'Bob the Builder' stories or watch a video clip. Then suggest that the children could recreate the stories they know.

▶ Allow time for the children to create their own stories in the building site.

▶ Talk with the children about how the different vehicles work.

▶ Make some STOP and GO signs for the small world using lolly sticks and card.

▶ Use construction bricks to make walls and structures.

▶ Talk about the different sorts of materials the builders use, how they behave when you pour or lift them, and what the materials are used for.

▶ Sing the theme tune to 'Bob the Builder' and encourage the children to make up their own verses.

▶ If you want to try another substance, try rice. Its texture is different and it's easier to clean up than sand!

Key words

digger	lorry	signposts	bricks
truck	bulldozer	lift	stop
cement mixer	tractor	carry	go
crane	safety helmet	heavy	
van	foreman	stones	

Bug World

Focus: Enjoy learning about creepy crawlies and their different habitats in this small world.

What you need:

▶ a builder's tray or equivalent large shallow container

▶ bark chippings or compost (buy new material from a garden centre)

▶ large logs, stones, sticks, leaves, branches and twigs

▶ plastic creepy crawlies (try to get realistic ones and those found in your locality)

▶ a selection of non-fiction books about insects and bugs

▶ hand lenses.

Contribution to Early Learning Goals for the EYFS

PRIME

Communication and Language ① ③

Physical Development ①

PSED ① ③

SPECIFIC

Mathematics ②

Understanding the world ① ②

Expressive arts and design ① ②

What to do:

Preparation

▶ You could go on a bug hunt in your garden, field, nature area or a local park to prepare children for this small world. Take some photos of the creatures you find and where they live.

▶ Let the children help to fill the tray with the bark chippings or compost, and arrange the logs, sticks, twigs etc. in the tray.

▶ Put the plastic bugs in a box or basket near the tray so the children can put them in the habitats on the logs or under the earth or stones.

▶ Arrange the books next to the tray.

Independent exploration

▶ Let the children explore the habitat and the creatures freely. They may not even know the names of the insects and spiders they are playing with. When you think they are ready, sit with them and talk generally about the habitats and minibeasts, referring to books and your photos if you can do this without interfering with the free play.

Ideas for adult-initiated activities:

▶ Use the books to identify individual bugs and match them with the photos from your bug hunt.

▶ Use hand lenses to explore the small world. If you have the tray set up outside, the children can extend this activity to exploring your garden or outdoor area.

▶ Sort and classify the insects according to colour, size, number of legs, wings etc.

▶ Try bringing a square of turf indoors for the children to explore with hand lenses. Any piece of turf is sure to have its own colonies of minibeasts to discover. (Don't cut the turf from a garden where pets may have been, and return the turf to the same place, complete with its minibeasts, when you have finished.)

Key words

insect names	shell	stick	under
bug	antennae	wood	cover
crawl	slide	camouflage	habitat
fly	log	magnify	protect
legs	twig	hide	

The Very Hungry Caterpillar

Focus: Learn the days of the week and the eating order of the story as you play.

What you need:

- a builder's tray or equivalent shallow container
- 'The Very Hungry Caterpillar' by Eric Carle
- bark chippings or compost from a garden centre
- large logs, sticks or twigs
- plastic or fabric caterpillars and butterflies
- plastic or silk flowers and plastic fruit and food as in the story.

Contribution to Early Learning Goals for the EYFS

PRIME

Communication and Language ① ③

Physical Development ①

PSED ① ③

SPECIFIC

Mathematics ②

Understanding the world ① ②

Expressive arts and design ① ②

What to do:

Preparation

▶ Read the story together, using the plastic fruit and insects as props.

▶ Let the children help to fill the tray with the bark chippings or compost and arrange the logs, sticks and twigs inside the tray.

▶ Add the flowers, caterpillars and butterflies to the tray, putting them on the logs, under the bark etc.

▶ Leave the plastic food in a basket nearby with the story and other books about insects.

Independent exploration

▶ Once you have read the story together, children will use their own imaginations to invent new versions as well as retelling the one they know. Younger children may like you to hold the book and turn the pages as they play the story, but don't impose at this stage, just let them play.

Ideas for adult-initiated activities:

▶ Use the story to help with revision of the order of the days of the week.

▶ Help the children to make up their own versions of the story. Older children may be able to use the same figures or additional insects and bugs to make up new versions.

▶ Work with the children to create an extra chapter for the book.

▶ Tell 'The Bad Tempered Ladybird', 'The Very Busy Spider', 'The Very Lonely Firefly' or 'The Very Quiet Cricket' — all by Eric Carle.

▶ Talk about the life cycle of a caterpillar and record notes on big sheets of paper.

▶ Try some still life drawing of the insects in the small world.

▶ Display the butterflies to draw or paint symmetrical pictures.

▶ Order a butterfly box from Insect Lore (www.insectlore.co.uk). They also have a huge range of insect-related kits, including bug eyes and butterfly wings for children to wear.

Key words

caterpillar	antennae	wood	pupa
butterfly	symmetrical	flowers	hatch
crawl	log	names of fruit	wings
fly	twig	life cycle	leaf
egg	stick	days of the week	

The Three Billy Goats Gruff

Focus: Trip trap through this small world and learn about geographical features.

What you need:

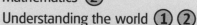

▶ a builder's tray, equivalent large shallow container or a square of carpet

▶ different versions of 'The Three Billy Goats Gruff' story

▶ large polished stones, twigs, sticks and leaves from your outdoor area

▶ greengrocer's grass or green fabric and blue fabric/plastic for the river

▶ construction materials

▶ small, medium and large plastic or fabric goats and a troll figure

▶ sticky notes and pencils.

Contribution to Early Learning Goals for the EYFS

PRIME

Communication and Language ① ③

Physical Development ①

PSED ① ③

SPECIFIC

Mathematics ②

Understanding the world ① ②

Expressive arts and design ① ②

What to do:

Preparation
- ▶ Tell the story of 'The Three Billy Goats Gruff'.
- ▶ Work with the children to create a landscape inside the tray using all the materials.
- ▶ Use construction materials to create a bridge over the blue fabric.
- ▶ Place the goats at one end of the bridge and the troll underneath the bridge ready for the story to begin.

Independent exploration
- ▶ Encourage the children to play out the version of the story that they have heard and some new versions they have made up.
- ▶ Play alongside if this doesn't inhibit their independence.

Ideas for adult-initiated activities:
- ▶ Read the story and allow time for the children to act out the story using the resources.
- ▶ Make some masks and play the story with children as the characters, lay a strip of blue cloth under a climbing frame or a plank bridge.
- ▶ Try offering a child the chance to be the narrator.
- ▶ Work together to discuss and create an extra chapter for the story.
- ▶ Talk about the geographical features of the small world and compare it to the natural environment of your setting.
- ▶ Offer labels, card and toothpicks or straws for the children to create labels for the natural features of the small world.
- ▶ Read the different versions of the text and ask children to identify similarities and differences.
- ▶ Tell some other familiar tales and talk about similarities and differences between stories.

Key words

log	meadow	mountain	goat
twig	grass	bridge	hooves
stick	water	big	troll
wood	river	medium	trip/trap
flowers	stream	small	

The Three Little Pigs

Focus: Huff and puff through this small world of a traditional tale.

What you need:

- a builder's tray or equivalent
- versions of 'The Three Little Pigs' text
- mother pig, three little pig figures and a wolf figure
- greengrocers' grass, twigs and straw
- small bricks or construction materials
- clipboards, paper and pencils, and a disposable camera.

Contribution to Early Learning Goals for the EYFS

PRIME

Communication and Language ① ③
Physical Development ①
PSED ① ③

SPECIFIC

Mathematics ②
Understanding the world ① ②
Expressive arts and design ① ②

What to do:

Preparation

▶ Tell the story of 'The Three Little Pigs'.

▶ Talk about the different houses the pigs made and how the children could make these from sticks, straws or bricks.

▶ Work with the children to lay the greengrocers' grass inside the tray and collect the remainder of the resources.

▶ Leave these beside the tray in boxes or baskets with glue, scissors etc. to help the construction.

Independent exploration

▶ Encourage the children to play out the version of the story that they have heard and make up new versions.

▶ Play alongside if this doesn't inhibit their independence, using some of the vocabulary below.

▶ Encourage the children to incorporate construction materials in their play, experimenting with different materials and structures.

Ideas for adult-initiated activities:

▶ Read a version of the text to the children while they are exploring.

▶ Ask the children to retell the story using the figures. Offer one child the chance to be the narrator.

▶ Talk with the children about what might happen in a new chapter of the book or a new adventure for the third little pig.

▶ Read the different versions of the text and ask children to identify the similarities and differences, or with adult support, compare the story to other fairy tales and identify their common features.

▶ Leave paper, pencils and clipboards near the small world for children to record what they have built in drawings or writing.

▶ Show the children how to use the camera and allow them to take photographs of what they create within the small world.

Key words

pig	twigs	build	button
piglet	bricks	strong	wind
wolf	blow	weak	adventure
straw	house	camera	chapter
sticks	down	photograph	

The Rainbow Fish

Focus: **Learn to share with the Rainbow Fish while playing with this small world.**

What you need:

▶ a water tray or large plastic aquarium
▶ a selection of plastic fish
▶ plastic aquarium plants, rocks, stones and aquarium decorations e.g. castles
▶ blue food colouring
▶ strips of silver foil and sequins
▶ a copy of 'The Rainbow Fish' story
▶ other Rainbow Fish stories.

Don't forget to provide aprons – this is a wet world!

Contribution to Early Learning Goals for the EYFS

PRIME
Communication and Language ①③
Physical Development ①
PSED ①③

SPECIFIC
Mathematics ②
Understanding the world ①②
Expressive arts and design ①②

What to do: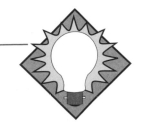

Preparation

▶ Tell the story of 'The Rainbow Fish'.
▶ Fill up your water tray or aquarium.
▶ Add some blue food colouring to the water.
▶ Add the fish, plants, stones etc.
▶ Sprinkle in some sequins and add silver foil strips.

Independent exploration

▶ The children will love this small world! Leave them to play uninterrupted and use the opportunity to observe them as they play out the story.
▶ If they invite you to join them, try to be a minor part of the story, letting them take the lead and asking simple open questions to establish what they want you to do.

Ideas for adult-initiated activities:

▶ Read the story and allow time for the children to act out the story using the resources.
▶ Relate the story to the children's own experiences of sharing.
▶ Have a separate cat litter tray of marbling inks next to the small world for the children to create their own underwater scene. Once dried, these could be used as a background for a Rainbow Fish collage.
▶ Continue the stories by reading other books in the Rainbow Fish series.
▶ Use the opportunity to collect some non-fiction books about fish and the sea.
▶ Use Google to find pictures, photos, videos and screensavers of tropical fish
▶ Visit a local pet shop, aquarium or zoo to see some real tropical fish.
▶ Collect pictures and books about Nemo.

Key words

rainbow	shimmer	kind	underwater
colour words	shiny	friends	tail
multi-coloured	fish	shell	fins
sea	scales	together	mouth
ocean	share	lonely	

Elmer

Focus: Elephants may not be as you expect in this small world jungle!

What you need:

▶ a builder's tray or equivalent large shallow container

▶ sand and water

▶ plastic elephant figures, including an Elmer figure (if possible)
– these can be bought in craft shops or could be made from
felt patches. You could even paint an elephant model with enamel paint!

▶ houseplants (e.g. a spider plant) to make a jungle and a lamp (for the sun)

▶ paper and coloured pencils, scissors and glue

▶ the 'Elmer' story by David McKee and a selection of other Elmer stories

▶ paint catalogues from DIY stores.

Contribution to Early Learning Goals for the EYFS

PRIME

Communication and Language ① ③

Physical Development ①

PSED ① ③

SPECIFIC

Mathematics ②

Understanding the world ① ②

Expressive arts and design ① ②

What to do:
Preparation
▶ Read the story of 'Elmer' with the children.
▶ Put sand inside the tray and leave space in the middle of the sand.
▶ Let the children fill the gap in the middle with water.
▶ Arrange the houseplants in one corner of the tray to create a jungle.
▶ Arrange the elephants and Elmer around the sand.
▶ If you can put a lamp somewhere safe, plug it in and put it near the small world tray.

Safety note:
MAKE SURE THE LAMP IS PLACED SAFELY AWAY FROM THE WATER.
DON'T USE EXTENSION LEADS.
HAVE AN ADULT SUPERVISING THIS ACTIVITY AT ALL TIMES WHEN THE LIGHT IS ON (REMEMBER, LIGHT BULBS GET VERY HOT!).

Independent exploration
▶ Allow plenty of time for free exploration in this small world. Most children love elephants and will make up their own stories about them.
▶ Play alongside if this doesn't inhibit their independence or creativity.

Ideas for adult-initiated activities:
▶ Reinforce colour words and the order of the rainbow colours.
▶ Ask the children how they could turn one of the elephants into Wilbur.
▶ Make or wear colourful jackets to recreate the Elmer Day parade.
▶ Sort the elephants into sets according to size etc.
▶ Locate hot countries on a map or globe.
▶ Give each child a square of colour from a paint catalogue. Ask them to find objects in your outdoor area that match that colour.
▶ Cut out the squares from a paint catalogue to make their own collages.
▶ Read other Elmer texts to the children.

Key words

colour words	elephant	plants	unhappy
rainbow	jungle	leaves	happy
multi-coloured	sand	friends	find
patchwork	water	rain	party
square	hot	lost	

Easter Bunny Hunt

Focus: Make a garden for an Easter egg hunt and wait for the Easter Bunny to come!

What you need:

- a builder's tray or equivalent
- greengrocer's grass or real turf, gravel, stones, small logs and bark
- silk, plastic or real flowers
- twigs, preferably with buds and leaves growing
- small world chicks, rabbits and small world people
- beads or tiny foil-covered eggs
- stories and fact books about spring, Easter, spring celebrations and growth.

I will need

Contribution to Early Learning Goals for the EYFS

PRIME

Communication and Language ① ③

Physical Development ①

PSED ① ③

SPECIFIC

Mathematics ②

Understanding the world ① ②

Expressive arts and design ① ②

What to do:
Preparation
▶ Talk to the children about spring and Easter, concentrating on new life. Explore some other cultures and traditions where eggs, rabbits and chickens feature in spring celebrations.
▶ Lay the greengrocer's grass inside the tray.
▶ Assemble the other resources in the tray.
▶ Introduce the idea of an Easter egg hunt in a garden. Talk about how to make a miniature garden in the tray.

Independent exploration
▶ The children will need plenty of time (and even some help) to construct a garden in the tray. Help by making suggestions and showing photos of different sorts of gardens. Encourage them to solve their own problems about standing things up, adding water, paths or gravel and making furniture, signs and notices.

Ideas for adult-initiated activities:
▶ Go for a spring walk in your garden or your neighbourhood. Look for signs of new growth on trees and bushes. Spot bulbs growing and birds nesting.
▶ Introduce the idea of a miniature egg hunt in the small world. Suggest that children could challenge each other to find hidden 'eggs' in the garden. Use oval beads or balls of foil so children aren't tempted to eat them.
▶ Have an Easter egg hunt in your garden or the park, or go egg rolling.
▶ Make hot cross buns or chocolate nests.
▶ Collect egg pictures and recipes. Try these sites for egg ideas:
   www.holidays.net/easter/eggs.html
   www.twingroves.district96.k12.il.us/Easter/Eggs.html
   or use a search engine for children's ideas and activities.

Key words

egg	path	round	patterns
chick	pond	search	shapes
rabbit	hide	game	rolling
flowers	under	spring	hot cross bun
leaves	behind	colours	

Here Comes Santa Claus!

Focus: Ho! Ho! Ho! in this seasonal small world.

What you need:

▶ a builder's tray or equivalent, such as a large square plant tray

▶ polystyrene wiggles or other shapes (or use paper shreddings, salt or flour for a more eco-friendly version)

▶ Santa, reindeer and snowmen figures (Christmas or cake decorations are ideal)

▶ a small artificial Christmas tree, tiny crackers, tree decorations and tinsel

▶ very small boxes for gifts and Christmas wrapping paper

▶ a tape recorder/CD player with a tape/CD of Christmas music.

Contribution to Early Learning Goals for the EYFS

PRIME

Communication and Language ① ③

Physical Development ①

PSED ① ③

SPECIFIC

Mathematics ②

Understanding the world ① ②

Expressive arts and design ① ②

What to do:

Preparation

▶ Tell a Christmas story or watch 'The Snowman' film.

▶ Work with the children to create a snowy landscape inside the tray using all the materials.

▶ Make some tiny parcels for Santa's sleigh and some houses for him to visit.

▶ Encourage the children to bring in their own Christmas music or to record Christmas songs they know.

Independent exploration

▶ Encourage the children to play out the story that they have heard and some new versions they have made up.

▶ Play alongside if this doesn't inhibit their independence.

Ideas for adult-initiated activities:

▶ Make an Advent calendar with 24 windows from 1st to 25th December.

▶ Make another small world to explore the Nativity story with Mary, Joseph, the shepherds and the Three Wise Men.

▶ Make a 'big' small world village or town with all the construction bricks you can gather (wooden, plastic, Lego, foam etc.). Take photos as you go. Use the model to extend children's play with Santa as he delivers across the town.

▶ If it snows (even if it's January or February) use the opportunity to make snow scenes indoors or out, using small world people. You could keep the things from this small world in a bag somewhere handy so you can get them out for the 'one day of snow' that most settings get.

▶ Look at books, videos, globes and atlases to find places where it is always cold and snowy. Talk about our seasons.

▶ Teach children how to use cameras, tape recorders and CD players independently.

Key words			
Christmas	snow	Rudolph	song/carol
Father Christmas	frost	tinsel	verse/chorus
tree	ice	play/stop/rewind	Santa
sledge	crackers	fast forward	
snap	reindeer	change	

Sliding and Skiing!

Focus: All children, especially boys, will love this play with skidding and sliding!

What you need:

- a large plastic tray, for example, a builder's tray or the lid to a sandpit/water tray
- trees, cars, bikes, small world people (a Playmobil snow set would be great)
- tin or plastic lids from jars and bottles for sledges
- sticks, ropes, play dough, card, paper, pens and scissors
- some shallow metal or plastic trays that will fit in a freezer.

I will need

Contribution to Early Learning Goals for the EYFS

PRIME

Communication and Language ① ③

Physical Development ①

PSED ① ③

SPECIFIC

Mathematics ②

Understanding the world ① ②

Expressive arts and design ① ②

What to do:

Preparation

(Warning! You will need reserves of ice to replace the melted ones!)

▶ In the winter, children love to slide and skid on icy puddles and paths. Use this as the stimulation for talking about skiing, sliding and skating.

▶ Try the idea when you are expecting a frosty night, so you can put the trays of water outside to freeze. If it isn't frosty, fill the shallow trays with water and put them in the freezer overnight. You could also freeze some bigger blocks of ice and some ice cubes to make different slopes and shapes. Prop some of the containers up so the water freezes in a sloping shape for skiing and sliding.

▶ Help the children to empty the frozen shapes into a shallow tray, and add some flour, shreddings or other fake snow if you like.

▶ Put the cars and people in a basket or box near the tray.

Independent exploration

▶ This setting probably needs an adult in attendance to help the children focus on the way things behave on slippery surfaces, but without restricting the fun!

Ideas for adult-initiated activities:

▶ You could make a ski slope or slalom course for small world people or a toboggan run for miniature sledges made from tops, plastic lids or other waterproof, slippery containers. Make skis for small world people from pieces of polystyrene trays or plastic cups.

▶ Work with the children to make signs and notices for the landscape, marking out paths and tracks and standing signs in play dough lumps for stability.

▶ Look at some footage or photos of winter sports: sledging, skiing and ski-jumping.

▶ If it snows or freezes, make an outdoor small world by leaving your water tray half full of water outside, propped up to make a slope.

Key words

slope	sledge	lake	slippery
slide	skis	melt/freeze	start/finish
skid	skates	ice/water	win
down	hill	snow	cold
fast/faster	pond	wheels	slow/slower

Some Other Ideas

Turf Exploration

▶ Use a builder's tray or equivalent large shallow container. Cut a square of turf from your own garden (where you can make sure it has not been fouled by pets).

▶ Give the children old forks and blunt knives to use for exploring this small world.

▶ Offer magnifying glasses, bug catchers and other collecting equipment for the small creatures they find.

▶ Return the turf and bugs after use.

Carry on Camping

▶ Either give children fabric, sticks and string to make their own tents or use suitable small tents (Action Man or other toys have these).

▶ Offer some figures and vehicles and play on a square of fake grass or on a lawn.

▶ Add to the interest by having a small world barbecue or camp fire (pretend of course!).

▶ Caravans and bikes will add to the fun (Lego bikes, Barbie caravans, speedboats etc.).

Spider

▶ Put some leaves and soil in an old builder's tray outside. Add some bits of wood, sticks etc.

▶ Leave somewhere it won't be disturbed for about a week. Either put it on a table outside or bring it indoors.

▶ Offer magnifying glasses and cameras to explore the minibeast world you have created.

▶ Remember to return the creatures to the garden when you have finished.

Seaside

▶ Make a seaside in a builder's tray. Use sand and water.

▶ Add stones, pebbles, shells and rocks.
Make seaweed from green and brown plastic bags.

▶ Offer some small world people to swim, sunbathe, sail or sit.

▶ Make chairs, sunbeds and add a few cocktail umbrellas.

▶ Use boxes to make cafes and ice cream parlours.

▶ Suggest a funfair, lifeboat or pier to extend the children's interests.

Down on the Farm

▶ Collect a range of brown, green, yellow and orange carpet tiles or carpet samples.

▶ Offer recycled materials for making hedges, fences and gates.

▶ Find some sticks or branches to make trees.

▶ Make some buildings from boxes.

▶ Offer playground chalk for drawing roads and yards.

▶ Collect up tractors, farm animals, people and other vehicles and play away!

Play a Story

Use small world to offer children opportunities to revisit and retell favourite stories. You could try:

Red Riding Hood

The Bear Hunt

Handa's Surprise

The Enormous Turnip

Goldilocks

This is the Bear

Noah's Ark

Happy Hedgehog Band

Three Bears.

Do it Yourself

And finally...

▶ Why not just provide materials and support for children to make their own small worlds?

▶ Let them bring TV and film character dolls to inhabit their own environments. Children will be very inventive with recycled materials – making furniture, shelters and vehicles for their stories. They won't worry if the characters are from different stories. The important thing is to support independent learning and thinking. Problem solving and collaborative working are often the result of negotiation. Children will love to bring their own figures from home to incorporate in the small world play.

▶ And remember, superhero play is much easier to handle if it takes place in a builder's tray!

If you are worried, or have rules about bringing toys from home, buy characters in sales, charity shops, 'pound' shops or second hand or collect freebies from restaurants. Parents may respond to an advert on a noticeboard for toys their children have grown out of.

WATFORD LRC

Hints and Tips

▶ Add mirrors to your small world at different heights. These will engage the children's attention and help them to view the world from different angles and perspectives. The mirrors will also lighten up dark areas and create the illusion of space. When a child sees their reflection, it will help to promote their self-awareness.

▶ Use multi-cultural people in your small worlds to promote the Early Learning Goal – 'understand that people have different needs, views, cultures and beliefs that need to be treated with respect'.

▶ Play topical music alongside your small world. Again, try to make this music multi-cultural and from a range of genres.

▶ Take photos of scenarios the children create within the small world. Keep a photo album of these pictures within the classroom. These can give other children ideas for their play and promote conversation with peers. The photos can also be used as a stimulus for writing during your literacy sessions.

▶ If it is a messy small world, remind the children to wear aprons or other protective clothing!

▶ If the children are working outside in cold weather, check to make sure they are warm enough. Children are sometimes so involved in the play that they don't realise they are cold.

Finding Resources

▶ Builders' trays can be purchased from DIY stores or from TTS supplies. (www.tts-group.co.uk or telephone 0800318686 for a free catalogue.)

▶ Greengrocer's grass can be found in educational supplies catalogues or try www.interiorlandscaping.co.uk for artificial grass.

▶ Look in 'pound' shops for tubs of large polished stones and packets of plastic insects.

▶ Visit your local garden centre for large plastic bugs, bark chippings and gravel.

▶ Your local pet shop will have small aquatic plants.

▶ Charity shops are a good source of low cost resources.

▶ At car boot sales, you can often purchase 'job lots' of very cheap items, especially if you tell the seller that the items are for an educational setting.

▶ Use supermarket own 'low cost' brands of jelly and shaving foam.

▶ Fake snow:
www.teachersource.com
www.shopping.com

▶ www.ebay.co.uk – a useful auction site to find resources for small world play boxes, story sacks and books.

▶ For seasonal activities, try:
www.christmastime.com
www.bbc.co.uk
www.familyfun.com

Books

▶ The Littlest Matryoshka by Corinne Demas; Bliss; ISBN 0786801530

▶ Fimbles and the Russian Doll; BBC books; ISBN 0563491531

▶ Bob's Busy Building Day; BBC books ISBN 1405900180

▶ The Very Hungry Caterpillar by Eric Carle; Board Book ISBN 0241003008

▶ The Three Billy Goats Gruff by B. Wade; ISBN 0749642262

▶ The Three Little Pig's Favourite Tales by Joan Stimson; ISBN 0721415385

▶ The Rainbow Fish by Marcus Pfister; ISBN 3314213883

▶ Elmer by David McKee; ISBN 0099697203

▶ The Easter Story by Heather Amery, Usborne Bible Tales; IBSN 0746033583

▶ The Christmas Story by Heather Amery, Usborne Bible Tales; IBSN 074604932

Dough Recipes

Long Life Dough

- ▶ 2 cups of plain flour
- ▶ 1 cup of salt
- ▶ 2 cups of water
- ▶ 2 tablespoons of vegetable oil
- ▶ 2 teaspoons of cream of tartar

Allow to cool and then knead well.

Store in an airtight container. For best results, keep in the fridge.

You can also place all the ingredients in a microwave dish and cook for about three and a half minutes, stirring after each minute.

Adding food colours and flavoured essences to this mixture makes for variety.

Chocolate Dough

Follow the recipe for long life playdough but replace one cup of flour with cocoa powder.

Coffee Dough

- ▶ a quarter of a cup of coffee granules
- ▶ 1 and a half cups of warm water
- ▶ 4 cups of flour
- ▶ 1 cup of salt

Dissolve the coffee in the warm water.

In a separate bowl, mix the flour and salt.

Make a hole in the mixture and add one cup of the coffee mixture.

Mix and add more of the coffee mixture until the mixture is smooth.

Gingerbread Dough

- ▶ 2 cups of flour
- ▶ 1 cup of salt
- ▶ 2 teaspoons of ground cinnamon
- ▶ 1 teaspoon of ground cloves
- ▶ 1 cup of water

Mix all the ingredients together to form dough.

Hot Cross Bun Dough

- ▶ 2 cups of wholemeal flour
- ▶ 1 cup of salt
- ▶ 2 teaspoons of mixed spice
- ▶ a sprinkling of currants
- ▶ 1 cup of water

Mix all the ingredients together to form dough.

To make the white crosses on top of the buns, use two cups of white flour, one cup of salt and one cup of water to make white dough.

Glitter Dough

- ▶ 3 cups of plain flour
- ▶ 1 cup of salt
- ▶ 1 tablespoon of cooking oil
- ▶ water for mixing
- ▶ 1 tablespoon of black, non-toxic children's paint or black food colouring
- ▶ silver glitter

Put all the dry ingredients in a bowl and stir together.

Add the paint and water to make stiff dough.

This dough will keep for up to a month in a plastic tub in the fridge.

Checklist for Small World Play Resources

Name of the small world ——————————————————

Contents list (what we have already got):

_____

_____

_____

_____

_____

Consumable resources (things that need replacing or topping up):

_____

_____

_____

_____

_____

Things we still need:

_____

_____

_____

_____

_____

Notes, contacts, free resources and ideas, including ideas suggested by the children:

_____

_____

_____

_____

_____